Spanish-English
DICTIONARY

Illustrated by
Rachael O'Neill

Translated by
Silvia Llaguno

CHRYSALIS CHILDREN'S BOOKS

This edition published in 2003 by
Chrysalis Children's Books,
an imprint of Chrysalis Books Group PLC,
The Chrysalis Building,
Bramley Road,
London W10 6SP

Every effort has been made to ensure none of the
recommended websites in this book is linked to
inappropriate material. However, due to the
ever-changing nature of the Internet, the publishers
regret they cannot take responsibility for future
content of these websites.

British Library Cataloguing in Publication Data for
this book is available from the British Library.

ISBN 1 903954 94 0 (hb)
ISBN 1 903954 95 9 (pb)

Printed and bound in China

Contents

About this book

This illustrated dictionary is just right if you are starting to learn Spanish. You will find that the picture index will help you translate a word, whether you know the Spanish or the English.

Masculine and feminine words

In Spanish, some words are masculine and some are feminine. **La** in front of a word means that it is feminine and **el** comes before a masculine word:

el conejo   (masculine singular)
the rabbit
la casa   (feminine singular)
the house

When the word is plural, it has **las** or **los** in front of it:
los conejos   (masculine plural)
las casas   (feminine plural)

Accents

In Spanish, you usually stress the second to last letter of the word. When a different letter is stressed, it is marked by an accent on the vowel:

á é í ó ú

The Spanish alphabet has an additional letter – **ñ**.

ñ is pronounced as 'nya'.

Useful Websites

For more on Spain and learning Spanish, check out these internet links:

A useful map of Spain showing the major cities: **www.map.freegk.com/spain/spain.php**

Some very famous Spanish paintings – for you to colour yourself:
www.cyberspain.com/colorme/iexplorer.htm

Find out about Mexico, a country in South America where Spanish is spoken: **www.elbalero.gob.mx/**

Learn to make some traditional Spanish dishes: **www.xmission.com/~dderhak/recipes.html**

Find out what children do in Ecuador, a Spanish-speaking country in South America, from this primary school's website: **http://ccph.com/ares/site/**. Look at Grade 4's page to see what it is like to have a pet monkey or capybara!

Check the Spanish you've learned with a word-matching game:
http://quizhub.com/quiz/f-spanish-v1.cfm

A good picture dictionary with some games and puzzles to check how good your Spanish is:
www.pdictionary.com/spanish/

Animals make the same noises in Spain and Britain, but we have different names for their noises! Find out what animal sounds are called in Spanish (and other languages):
www.georgetown.edu/cball/animals/animals.html

Try hangman in Spanish and other puzzles to see how much you know:
www.linguaweb.ndirect.co.uk/pages/spanlev1.htm

Say something hard! Spanish tongue twisters from different countries where Spanish is spoken:
www.uebersetzung.at/twister/es.htm. Click on the number to see it in English.

Internet Safety

Always follow these guidelines for a fun and safe journey through cyberspace:

1. Ask your parents for permission before you go online.
2. Spend time with your parents online, and show them your favourite sites.
3. Post your family's e-mail address, even if you have your own (only give your personal address to someone you trust).
4. Do not reply to e-mails if you feel they are strange or upsetting.
5. Do not use your real surname while you are online.
6. Never arrange to meet 'cyber friends' in person without your parents' permission.
7. Never give out your password.
8. Never give out your home address or telephone number.
9. Do not send scanned pictures of yourself unless your parents approve.
10. Leave a website straight away if you find something that is offensive or upsetting. Talk to your parents about it.

Diccionario Ilustrado
Picture Dictionary

Inglés – Español
English – Spanish

Aa

acorn
la bellota

aerial
la antena

aeroplane
el avión

airport
el aeropuerto

alligator
el caimán

alphabet
el alfabeto

ambulance
la ambulancia

angler
el pescador de caña

anorak
el anorak

antlers
las astas

apple
la manzana

aqualung
la botella de oxígeno

armband
los brazadores

armchair
el sillón

armour
la armadura

arrow
la flecha

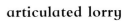

articulated lorry
el camión semi-remolque

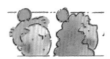
audience
los espectadores

autumn
el otoño

Bb

baby
el bebé

back door
la puerta trasera

balloon
el globo

7

Aa Bb Cc Dd Ee Ff Gg Hh Ii Jj Kk Ll Mm Nn Oo Pp Qq Rr Ss Tt Uu Vv Ww Xx Yy Zz

banana
el plátano

bandage
la venda

bank
el banco

bar
la reja

barn
el granero

baseball bat
el bate de beisbol

bath
la bañera

bath mat
la alfombrilla de baño

bath towel
la toalla de baño

bathroom scales
la báscula

beach
la playa

beach ball
la pelota de playa

beach towel
la toalla de playa

beak
el pico

beaker
el cubilete

bedding
la cama

belt
el cinturón

bench
el banco

berry
la fruta del bosque

bicycle
la bicicleta

bird
el pájaro

bird table
la mesa para pájaros

biscuit tin
la caja de galletas

black
negro (m)
negra (f)

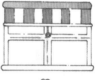
blind
el estor

blossom
las flores

blue
azul

board game
el juego de mesa

boat
el barco

bone
el hueso

bonfire
la fogata

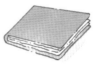
book
el libro

8

bookcase
las estanterias

boot
las botas

border
el parterre

bottom
la parte de abajo

bow
el arco

bow
el lazo

bowl
la ensaladera

box
la caja

braces
los tirantes

branch
la rama

bread
el pan

brick
el ladrillo

bricklayer
el albañil

bridge
el puente

broom
la escoba

broomstick
el palo de escoba

brown
marrón

bucket
el cubo

buckle
la hebilla

bud
el capullo

budgerigar
el periquito

builder
el obrero

building block
el juego de
construcción

bull
el toro

bulldozer
el tractor nivelador

bus
el autobús

bus driver
el conductor de
autobús

bus stop
la parada del
autobús

bush
el matorral

butter
la mantequilla

button
el botón

buttonhole
el ojal

Cc

cabinet
el armarito

café
la cafetería

cage
la jaula

cake
el pastel

calf
el ternero

camel
el camello

canal
el canal

canal boat
el barco de canal

candle
la vela

candlestick
el sujeta-velas

cannon
el cañón

canoe
la canoa

car
el coche

car park
el aparcamiento

card
la tarjeta de felicitación

cardboard model
la maqueta

cardigan
la chaqueta de lana

carpenter
el carpintero

carpet
la alfombra

carriage
el vagón

castle
el castillo

cat flap
la gatera

cauldron
la olla

cauliflower
la coliflor

cave
la cueva

cement mixer
la mezcladora de cemento

cereal
los cereales

chair
la silla

chalk
la tiza

chalkboard
la pizarra

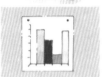
chart
el diagrama

cheese
el queso

cheetah
el guepardo

chest of drawers
la comoda

chick
el pollito

chips
las patatas fritas

circle
el círculo

clam
la almega

claw
la zarpa

clay
la arcilla

cliff
el acantilado

climbing frame
los hierros
para trepar

cloak
la capa

clock
el reloj

clown
el payaso

coat
el abrigo

coconut
el coco

coffee
el café

coffee table
la mesa de café

collar
el cuello

colouring book
el libro de colorear

comic
el tebeo

compact disc player
el lector de discos
compactos

compressor
la compresora

computer
el ordenador

concrete mixer
le mezcladora de
granito

cooker
la cocina

coral
el coral

cord
el cordón

cotton wool
el algodón

cow
la vaca

cowboy outfit
el traje de vaquero

cowshed
el pajar

cracker
la sorpresa
Navideña

crane
la grúa

crayon
el lápiz de colores

crisps
las patatas fritas

crocus
la flor del azafrán

crossing
el paso de zebra

crown
la corona

cube
el cubo

cucumber
el pepino

cuff
el puño

cup
la taza

cupboard
la alacena

curtain pole
la barra de cortina

curtain
la cortina

Dd

daffodil
el narciso

dandelion
el diente de león

deckchair
la butaca de playa

deer
el ciervo

desk
la mesa de escribir

dice
los dados

digger
la excavadora

ditch
la fosa

diver
el buzo

doctor's bag
el maletín de
médico

doctor's outfit
el disfraz de médico

doll's clothes
los vestiditos de
muñeca

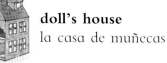
doll's house
la casa de muñecas

dolphin
el delfín

down
abajo

dragon
el dragón

draining board
la escurridera

drawer
el cajón

drawing
el dibujo

drawing pin
la chincheta

dress
el vestido

dressing gown
la bata

drink
la bebida

driver
el conductor

drum
el tambor

duck
el pato

duckling
el patito

duck pond
el lago de patos

dumper truck
el camión vertedero

dungarees
el mono

Ee

ear muffs
las orejeras

eel
la anguila

egg
el huevo

elephant
el elefante

enchanted wood
el bosque encantado

evergreen tree
el árbol de hoja perenne

Ff

face mask
las gafas de buzo

fairy
el hada

fairy lights
las luces de Navidad

family
la familia

fan
el ventilador

farmer
el granjero

farmyard
el corral

fat
gordo/a

ferry boat
el ferry

fin
la aleta

fire
el fuego

fire engine
el coche de
bomberos

fireguard
el guarda fuegos

fireplace
la chimenea

flag
la bandera

flamingo
el flamingo

flannel
la toalla de baño

flashcard
la tarjeta
nemotécnica

flipper
las aletas

floor tile
el suelo de baldosas

flower bed
el parterre

flowerpot
el tiesto

foal
el potro

food bowl
el cuenco de
comida

football
el balón de fútbol

fork
el tenedor

fossil
el fósil

freezer
el congelador

fridge
el frigorífico

frying pan
la sartén

fur
el pelaje

Gg

garage
el garage

garden birds
los pájaros de
jardín

garden fork
la horca

garlic
el ajo

gate
la puerta

gerbil
el jerbo

ghost
el fantasma

14

giant
el gigante

giraffe
la girafa

glove
el guante

glove puppet
la marioneta de trapo

gnome
el nomo

goat
la cabra

goggles
las gafas de bucear

goose
el ganso

gosling
el pequeño ganso

grape
la uva

green
verde

grey
gris

guard
el guardia de estación

guinea pig
el conejo de Indias

guitar
la guitarra

Hh

hamburger
la hamburguesa

hamster
el hamster

hamster house
la jaula del hamster

handkerchief
el pañuelo

handlebars
el manillar

hanger
la percha

happy
contento/a

hard
duro/a

hat
el sombrero

hay
el heno

helicopter
el helicóptero

helmet
el casco

hen
la gallina

hen house
el gallinero

15

hippopotamus
el hipopótamo

honey
la miel

hood
la capucha

horn
el cuerno

horse
el caballo

hose
la manguera

hospital
el hospital

hot air balloon
el globo

hot dog
el perrito caliente

hotel
el hotel

house
la casa

hovercraft
el hidrofoil

hutch
la conejera

Ii

ice
el hielo

ice-cream
el helado

island
la isla

Jj

jam
la mermelada

jeans
los vaqueros

jellyfish
la medusa

jester
el bufón

jigsaw puzzle
el puzle

jug
la jarra

juice
el zumo

jumper
el jersey

Kk

kangaroo
el canguro

king
el rey

kite
la cometa

kitten
el gatito

knickers
las bragas

knife
el cuchillo

knight
el caballero

Ll

laces
los cordones

ladder
la escalera

lake
el lago

lamb
el cordero

lamp
la lámpara

lamp post
la farola

lampshade
la pantalla de
la lámpara

laundry basket
la cesta de la ropa
sucia

lawn
el césped

lawnmower
la corta-césped

lead
la correa

leaf
la hoja

Lego
el juego de Lego

leopard
el leopardo

leotard
la malla

library
la biblioteca

lifejacket
el chaleco salvavidas

light
el foco de luz

lighthouse
el faro

lion
el león

lioness
la leona

lion cub
el cachorro de león

lizard
la lagartija

llama
la llama

loader
la cargadora

lobster
la langosta

long
largo (m)/larga (f)

loudspeaker
el altavoz

Mm

magazine
la revista

magician
el mago

make-up
el maquillaje

map
el mapa

mantlepiece
la repisa de la
chimenea

marble
las canicas

margarine
la margarina

mast
el mástil

mince
la carne picada

mirror
el espejo

mist
la niebla

mitten
las manoplas

moat
el foso

monkey
el mono

monster
el monstruo

moon
la luna

motor boat
la lancha motora

motorbike
la motocicleta

motorway
la autopista

mushroom
los champiñones

Nn

nailbrush
el cepillo de uñas

narrow
estrecho (m)
estrecha (f)

nature table
la exposición de
Naturaleza

nest
el nido

nesting box
la casa de pájaros

net
la red

new
nuevo (m)
nueva (f)

newspaper
el periódico

Noah's ark
el Arca de Noé

notice
el cartel

numbers
los números

nurse's outfit
el disfraz de
enfermera

Oo

oak tree
el roble

oar
el remo

octopus
el pulpo

oil
el aceite

old
viejo (m)
vieja (f)

onion
la cebolla

orange
naranja

orange
la naranja

orchard
el frutal

ostrich
el avestruz

oven
el horno

overalls
el mono

owl
el buho

oyster
la ostra

Aa Bb Cc Dd Ee Ff Gg Hh Ii Jj Kk Ll Mm Nn Oo Pp Qq Rr Ss Tt Uu Vv Ww Xx Yy Zz

Pp

padlock
el candado

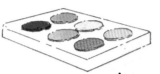
paint
las pinturas

paintbrush
el pincel

painting
el cuadro

pants
los calzoncillos

paper chain
la cadena

paper cup
la taza de papel

paper flower
la flor de papel

paper hat
la corona de papel

paper napkin
la servilleta de papel

paper plate
el plato de papel

parachute
el paracaidas

parcel
el paquete

park keeper
el guardia del parque

parrot
el loro

party dress
el vestido de fiesta

party squeaker
el matasuegras

paste
la cola

paste brush
la brocha de encolar

pavement
la acera

paw
la pata

pea
el guisante

peanut
el cacahuete

pear
la pera

pebble
el guijarro

pedal
el pedal

peg
el colgador

pelican
el pelícano

pencil
el lapicero

pencil case
el estuche de lapiceros

pepper
la pimienta

pet/cat food
la comida de perro/gato

petrol pump
la surtidora de gasolina

petrol station
la gasolinera

photograph
la photographia

picnic
el picnic

picnic basket
la cesta de picnic

pier
el muelle

pig
el cerdo

pigeon
la paloma

piglet
el cochinillo

pig sty
la pocilga

pillow
la almohada

pinafore dress
el delantal

pinboard
el corcho

pink
rosa

pirate
el pirata

Plasticine
la plasticina

plate
el plato

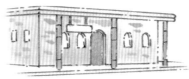
platform
el andén

playground
el area de juegos

plimsoll
las playeras

plug
el tapon

plum
la ciruela

plume
la pluma

pneumatic drill
la taladradora

pocket
el bolsillo

police officer
el policia

21

pond
el estanque

postman
postwoman
el cartero
la cartera

potato
la patata

pram
el cochecito de
bebés

present
el regalo

primrose
la primavera

prince
el príncipe

princess
la príncesa

puppy
el cachorro de
perro

purple
púrpura/violeta

pushchair
la sillita de niños

pyjamas
el pijama

Qq

queen
la reina

quilt
la colcha

Rr

rabbit
el conejo

radiator
el radiador

radio
la radio

railing
la cerca

railway
el ferrocarril

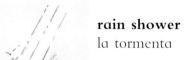

rain shower
la tormenta

rainbow
el arco-iris

rake
el rastrillo

rattle
el sonajero

ray fish
la raya

reader
la lectora (f)
el lector (m)

record player
el toca-discos

rectangle
el rectángulo

red
rojo (m)
roja (f)

reed
la caña

remote control
el mando a distancia

rhinoceros
el rinoceronte

ribbon
el lazo

rice
el arroz

river
el río

river bank
la orilla del río

rock garden
el jardín de rocas

rocking chair
la mecedora

roller skates
los patines

roof
el techo

rose
la rosa

rotor blade
la hélice

roundabout
el tio-vivo

rowing boat
el barco de remos

rubber
la goma de borrar

rubbish bin
la papelera

rug
la alfombra

ruler
la regla

Ss

sad
triste

saddle
el sillín

safety hat
el casco

sail
la vela

sailing boat
el barco de vela

salt
la sal

sand
la arena

sandal
la sandalia

sandcastle
el castillo de arena

sandpit
la fosa de arena

satchel
le cartera

scaffolding
el andamio

scarecrow
el espanta-pájaros

scarf
la bufanda

scissors
las tijeras

sea
el mar

sea anemone
la anémona de mar

seagull
la gaviota

seahorse
el caballito de mar

seal
la foca

seaweed
las algas

seesaw
el balancín

settee
el sofá

shampoo
el champú

shark
el tiburón

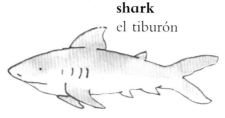

shed
la cabaña

sheep
la oveja

sheepdog
el perro pastor

sheet
la sábana

shell
la concha

shelter
la parada
de autobus
cubierta

shield
el escudo

shirt
la camisa

shoal
el banco de peces

shoe
el zapato

shop
la tienda

short
corto (m)
corta (f)

short
pequeño (m)
pequeña (f)

shower
la ducha

24

shower cap
el gorro de ducha

shower curtain
la cortina de baño

shrimp
la gamba

shrub
el arbusto

sink
el fregadero

skateboard
el patinete

skip
el vertedero

skipping rope
la cuerda de saltar

skirt
la falda

sledge
el trineo

sleeve
la manga

slide
el tobogán

slipper
las zapatillas de casa

slope
el terraplén

snake
la serpiente

snorkel
el tubo respiratorio

snow
la nieve

snowball
la bola de nieve

snowflake
el copo de nieve

snowman
el muñeco de nieve

soap
el jabón

soap dish
la jabonera

sock
el calcetín

soft
blando (m)
blanda (f)

soup
la sopa

spacecraft
la nave espacial

spade
la pala

spaghetti
los espaguetis

sphere
la esfera

spice
las especias

sponge
la esponja

spoon
la cuchara

25

spring
le primavera

square
el cuadrado

squash
el concetrado de zumo

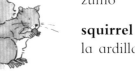
squirrel
la ardilla

stable
la cuadra

star
la estrella

starfish
la estrella de mar

station
la estación

steamroller
la apisonadora

steering wheel
el volante

step
el escalón

stethoscope
el estetoscopio

stool
el taburete

straw
la paja

streamer
la serpentina

sucker
la ventosa

sugar
el azucar

summer
el verano

sun
el sol

suntan lotion
el bronceador

sunglasses
las gafas de sol

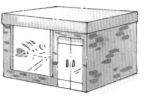
supermarket
el supermercado

surfboard
la tabla de surf

sweatshirt
la sudadera

sword
la espada

swordfish
el pez espada

Tt

table
la mesa

tablecloth
el mantel

tail
la cola

tall
grande

tap
el grifo

tape recorder
la grabadora

target
la diana

tarmac
el asfalto

taxi
el taxi

teacher
la profesora (f)
el profesor (m)

telegraph pole
el palo telegráfico

telephone
el teléfono

television
la televisión

tennis ball
la pelota de tenis

tennis court
la pista de tenis

tent
la tienda de
campaña

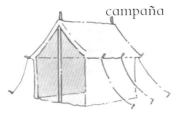

tentacle
el tentáculo

terrace
el terrazo

Thermos flask
el termo

thin
flaco (m)
flaca (f)

ticket
el billete

tiger
el tigre

tights
los leotardos

tile
los azulejos

tipper truck
el camión vertedero

toadstool
la seta venenosa

toaster
la tostadora de pan

toilet
el wáter

toilet paper
el papel higiénico

toilet seat
la tara del wáter

tomato
el tomate

toothbrush
el cepillo de dientes

toothpaste
la pasta dentífrica

top
la parte de arriba

toy farm
la granja de juguete

treasure
el tesoro

toy shop
la tienda de juguete

top hat
el sombrero de copa

tree stump
el tocón

torch
la linterna

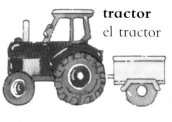

tractor
el tractor

triangle
el triángulo

tortoise
la tortuga

traffic lights
el semáforo

tricycle
el triciclo

towel rail
el toallero

traffic warden
la guardia de
tráfico (f)
el guardia de
tráfico (m)

tower block
el bloque de pisos

trough
el abrevadero

town hall
el ayuntamiento

trailer
el remolque

trowel
la paleta

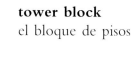
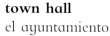

train
el tren

truck
el camión

toy boat
el barquito
de juguete

train set
el trenecito de
juguete

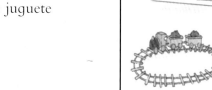

T-shirt
la camiseta

toy box
el baúl de los
juguetes

trainers
las zapatillas
de deporte

trunk
la trompa

28

tube
el tubo

tunnel
el tunel

turtle
la tortuga marina

tusk
el colmillo

tyre
el neumático

Uu

umbrella
la sombrilla

unicorn
el unicornio

up
arriba

Vv

van
el todo-terreno

vase
el jarrón

vest
la camiseta interior
(sin mangas)

video recorder
el aparato de video

vinegar
el vinagre

Ww

wall
el muro

walrus
la morsa

wardrobe
el armario

washbasin
el lavabo

washing machine
la lavadora

wastepaper bin
la papelera

watch
el reloj de pulsera

water bottle
la botella de agua

waterfall
la fuente

waterlily
el nenúfar

wave
la ola

weed
la mala hierba

wet suit
el traje de buzo

whale
la ballena

wheel
la rueda

wheelbarrow
la carretilla

wheelchair
la silla de ruedas

white
blanco (m)
blanca (f)

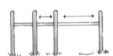
wide
ancho

wild garden
el jardín agreste

windbreak
el parapeto

window
la ventana

window box
la jardinera

window cleaner
el limpia-ventanas

windowsill
el poyete de la ventana

windscreen
el para-brisas

windsurfer
la tabla de windsurf

wing
el ala

winter
el invierno

wire netting
la red metálica

witch
la bruja

wizard
el mago

worktop
la encimera

wreck
el naufragio

Xx

xylophone
el xilófono

Yy

yacht
el yate

yellow
amarillo (m)
amarilla (f)

yo-yo
el yo-yo

Zz

zebra
la zebra

zip
la cremallera

Picture Dictionary
Diccionario Ilustrado

Spanish – English
Español – Inglés

Aa

abajo
down

el abrevadero
trough

el abrigo
coat

el acantilado
cliff

el aceite
oil

la acera
pavement

el aeropuerto
airport

el ajo
garlic

el ala
wing

la alacena
cupboard

el albañil
bricklayer

la aleta
fin

las aletas
flipper

el alfabeto
alphabet

la alfombra
carpet

la alfombra
rug

la alfombrilla de baño
bath mat

las algas
seaweed

el algodón
cotton wool

la almeja
clam

la almohada
pillow

el altavoz
loudspeaker

amarillo
yellow

la ambulancia
ambulance

ancho
wide

el andamio
scaffolding

el andén
platform

la anémona de mar
sea anemone

la anguila
eel

el anorak
anorak

la antena
aerial

el aparato de video
video recorder

el aparcamiento
car park

la apisonadora
steamroller

el árbol de hoja perenne
evergreen tree

el arbusto
shrub

el arca de Noé
Noah's ark

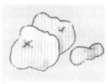
la arcilla
clay

el arco
bow

el arco-iris
rainbow

la ardilla
squirrel

el area de juego
playground

la arena
sand

la armadura
armour

el armario
wardrobe

el armarito
cabinet

arriba
up

el arroz
rice

el asfalto
tarmac

el asiento
saddle

las astas
antlers

el autobús
bus

la autopista
motorway

el avestruz
ostrich

el avión
aeroplane

el ayuntamiento
town hall

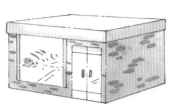
el azucar
supermarket

azul
blue

los azulejos
tile

Bb

el balancín
seesaw

la ballena
whale

**el balón
de fútbol**
football

el banco
bank

el banco
bench

**el banco
de peces**
shoal

la bandera
flag

la bañera
bath

el barco
boat

el barco de canal
canal boat

**el barco
de juguete**
toy boat

el barco de vela
sailing boat

**el barquito
de remos**
rowing boat

la barra
bar

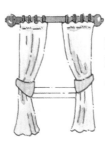
**la barra de
la cortina**
curtain pole

la báscula
bathroom scales

33

la bata
dressing gown

el bate de beisbol
baseball bat

el baúl de juguetes
toy box

el bebé
baby

la bebida
drink

la bellota
acorn

la biblioteca
library

la bicicleta
bicycle

el billete
ticket

blanco (m) blanca (f)
white

blando (m) blanda (f)
soft

el bloque de pisos
tower block

el bol de comida
food bowl

la bola de nieve
snowball

el bolsillo
pocket

el bosque encantado
enchanted wood

la bota
boot

la botella de agua
water bottle

la botella de oxígeno
aqualung

el botón
button

las bragas
knickers

los brazadores
armband

el bronceador
suntan lotion

la bruja
witch

la bufanda
scarf

el bufón
jester

el buho
owl

la butaca de playa
deckchair

Aa Bb Cc Dd Ee Ff Gg Hh Ii Jj Kk Ll Mm Nn Oo Pp Qq Rr Ss Tt Uu Vv Ww Xx Yy Zz

el buzo
diver

Cc

el caballero
knight

el caballito de mar
seahorse

el caballo
horse

la cabaña
shed

la cabra
goat

el cacahuete
peanut

el cachorro de león
lion cub

el cachorro de perro
puppy

el café
coffee

la cafetería
café

el caimán
alligator

la caja
box

la caja de galletas
biscuit tin

el cajón
drawer

el calcetín
sock

los calzoncillos
pants

la cama
bedding

el camello
camel

el camión
truck

el camión de descarga
dumper truck

el camión semi-remolque
articulated lorry

el camión vertedero
tipper truck

la camisa
shirt

la camiseta
T-shirt

la camiseta interior (sin mangas)
vest

la caña
reed

el canal
canal

el candado
padlock

el canguro
kangaroo

la canica
marble

la canoa
canoe

el cañón
cannon

la capa
cloak

la capucha
hood

el capullo
bud

la cargadora
loader

la carne picada
mince

el carpintero
carpenter

la carretilla
wheelbarrow

el cartel
notice

la cartera
satchel

**el cartero (m)
la cartera (f)**
postman
postwoman

la casa
house

la casa de muñecas
doll's house

la casa de pájaros
nesting box

el casco
helmet

el casco
safety hat

el castillo
castle

el castillo de arena
sandcastle

la cebolla
onion

el cepillo de dientes
toothbrush

el cepillo de uñas
nailbrush

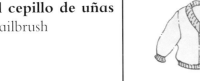
la chaqueta de lana
cardigan

el cochecito de bebé
pram

la cerca
railing

la chimenea
fireplace

el cerdo
pig

la chincheta
drawing pin

el cochinillo
piglet

los cereales
cereal

el ciervo
deer

la cocina
cooker

el césped
lawn

la cigala
lobster

el coco
coconut

la cesta de picnic
picnic basket

el cinturón
belt

la cola
paste brush

la cesta de la ropa
laundry basket

el círculo
circle

la cola
paste

el chaleco salvavidas
lifejacket

la ciruela
plum

la cola
tail

el champiñón
mushroom

el coche
car

la colcha
quilt

el champú
shampoo

el coche de bomberos
fire engine

el colgador
peg

37

la coliflor
cauliflower

el colmillo
tusk

la cometa
kite

**la comida de
perro/gato**
pet/cat food

la comoda
chest of drawers

la compresora
compressor

**el conductor de
autobús**
bus driver

la conejera
hutch

el conejo
rabbit

**el concetrado
de zumo**
squash

la concha
shell

el conductor
driver

el conejo de Indias
guinea pig

el congelador
freezer

**contento (m)
contenta (f)**
happy

el copo de nieve
snowflake

el coral
coral

el corcho
pinboard

el cordero
lamb

el cordón
cord

los cordones
lace

la corona
crown

**la corona de
papel**
paper hat

el corral
farmyard

la correa
lead

**la cortadora de
césped**
lawnmower

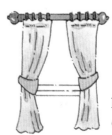
la cortina
curtain

la cortina de baño
shower curtain

corto (m) corta (f)
short

la cremallera
zip

el cuadrado
square

el cuadro
painting

el cubilete
beaker

el cubo
bucket

el cubo
cube

la cuchara
spoon

el cuchillo
knife

el cuello
collar

la cuerda de saltar
skipping rope

el cuerno
horn

la cueva
cave

Dd

el dado
dice

el delantal
pinafore dress

el delfin
dolphin

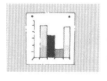
el diagrama
chart

la diana
target

el dibujo
drawing

el diente de león
dandelion

el disfraz de enfermera
nurse's outfit

el disfraz de médico
doctor's outfit

el disfraz de vaquero
cowboy outfit

el dragón
dragon

la ducha
shower

duro (m) dura (f)
hard

39

Ee

el elefante
elephant

la encimera
worktop

la ensaladera
bowl

la escalera
ladder

el escalón
step

la escoba
broom

el escudo
shield

el escurridero
draining board

la esfera
sphere

la espada
sword

los espaguetis
spaghetti

el espanta-pájaros
scarecrow

las especias
spice

los espectadores
audience

el espejo
mirror

la esponja
sponge

el establo
cowshed

el establo
stable

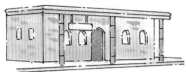

la estación
station

el estanque
pond

**el estanque
de patos**
duck pond

la estanteria
bookcase

el estetoscopio
stethoscope

el estor
blind

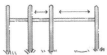

**estrecho (m)
estrecha (f)**
narrow

la estrella
star

**la estrella
de mar**
starfish

el estuche
pencil case

la excavadora
digger

Ff

la falda
skirt

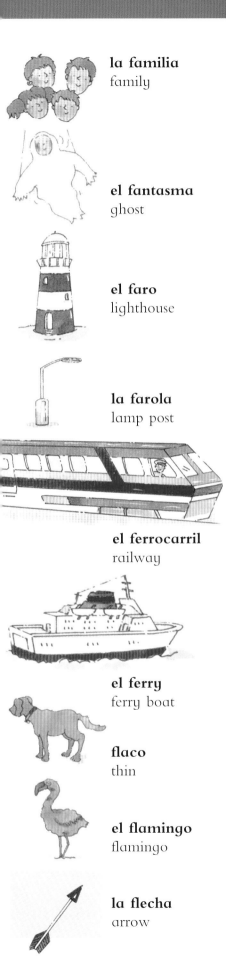

la familia
family

el fantasma
ghost

el faro
lighthouse

la farola
lamp post

el ferrocarril
railway

el ferry
ferry boat

flaco
thin

el flamingo
flamingo

la flecha
arrow

la flor de papel
paper flower

la flor del azafrán
crocus

las flores
blossom

la foca
seal

el foco de la luz
light

la fogata
bonfire

la fosa
ditch

el fósil
fossil

el foso
moat

el foso de arena
sandpit

la fotografía
photograph

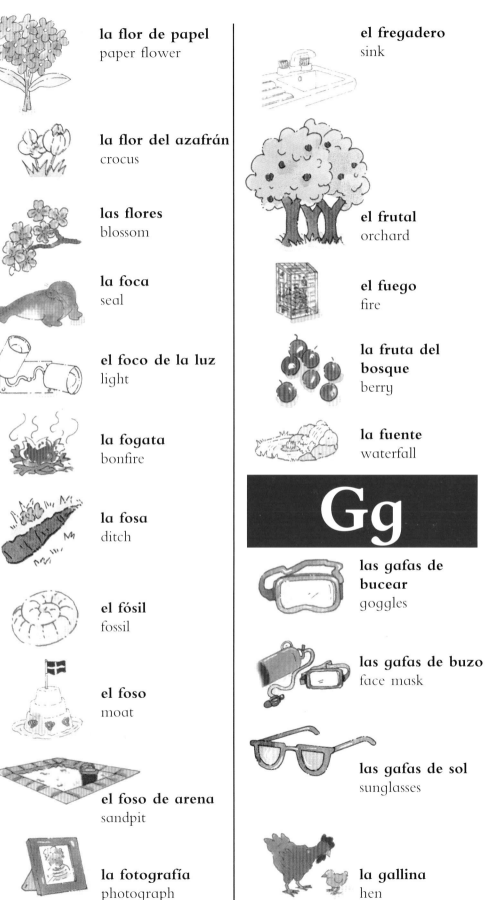

el fregadero
sink

el frutal
orchard

el fuego
fire

la fruta del bosque
berry

la fuente
waterfall

Gg

las gafas de bucear
goggles

las gafas de buzo
face mask

las gafas de sol
sunglasses

la gallina
hen

41

el gallinero
hen house

la gamba
shrimp

el ganso
goose

el ganso pequeño
gosling

el garage
garage

la gasolinera
petrol pump

la gasolinera
petrol station

la gatera
cat flap

el gatito
kitten

la gaviota
seagull

el gigante
giant

la girafa
giraffe

el globo
balloon

el globo
hot air balloon

**la goma
de borrar**
rubber

**gordo (m)
gorda (f)**
fat

el gorro de ducha
shower cap

grande
tall

el granero
barn

**la granja de
juguete**
toy farm

el granjero
farmer

el grifo
tap

gris
grey

la grúa
crane

el guante
glove

el guarda fuego
fireguard

**el guardia de
estación**
guard

**el guardia de
tráfico (m)
la guardia de
tráfico (f)**
traffic warden

el guardia del parque
park keeper

el guepardo
cheetah

el guijarro
pebble

la guirlanda
paper chain

el guisante
pea

la guitarra
guitar

Hh

el hada
fairy

la hamburguesa
hamburger

el hamster
hamster

la hebilla
buckle

el helado
ice-cream

la hélice
rotor blade

el helicóptero
helicopter

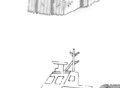
el heno
hay

el hidrofoil
hovercraft

el hielo
ice

los hierros para trepar
climbing frame

el hipopótamo
hippopotamus

la hoja
leaf

el horno
oven

el hospital
hospital

el hotel
hotel

el hueso
bone

el huevo
egg

Ii

el invierno
winter

la isla
island

Jj

el jabón
soap

la jabonera
soap dish

43

el jardin agreste
wild garden

el juego de mesa
board game

la lavadora
washing machine

el jardín de rocas
rock garden

Ll

el lazo
bow

la jardinera
window box

el ladrillo
brick

el lazo
ribbon

la jarra
jug

la lagartija
lizard

el lector de discos compactos
compact disc player

el jarrón
vase

el lago
lake

la lectora (f)
el lector (m)
reader

la jaula
cage

la lámpara
lamp

el león
lion

la leona
lioness

la jaula del hamster
hamster house

la lancha motora
motor boat

el leopardo
leopard

el jerbo
gerbil

el lapicero
pencil

los leotardos
tights

el jersey
jumper

el lápiz de colores
crayon

el libro
book

el juego de construcción
building block

largo (m)
larga (f)
long

el libro de colorear
colouring book

el juego de Lego
Lego

el lavabo
washbasin

el limpia-ventanas
window cleaner

la linterna
torch

la llama
llama

el loro
parrot

las luces de Navidad
fairy lights

la luna
moon

Mm

el magnetófono
tape recorder

el mago
magician

el mago
wizard

la mala hierba
weed

el maletín de médico
doctor's bag

la malla
leotard

el mando a distancia
remote control

la manga
sleeve

la manguera
hose

el manillar
handlebars

la manopla
mitten

el mantel
tablecloth

la mantequilla
butter

la manzana
apple

el mapa
map

la maqueta
cardboard model

el maquillaje
make-up

el mar
sea

la margarina
margarine

la marioneta de trapo
glove puppet

marrón
brown

el mástil
mast

el matasuegras
party squeaker

el matorral
bush

la mecedora
rocking chair

la medusa
jellyfish

la mermelada
jam

la mesa
table

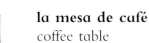
la mesa de café
coffee table

la mesa de escribir
desk

la mesa de objetos naturales
nature table

la mesa de pájaros
bird table

el mezclador de granito
concrete mixer

la mezcladora de cemento
cement mixer

la miel
honey

el mono
dungarees

el mono
monkey

el mono
overalls

el monstruo
monster

la morsa
walrus

la motocicleta
motorbike

el muelle
pier

el muñeco de nieve
snowman

el muro
wall

Nn

naranja
orange

la naranja
orange

el narciso
daffodil

el naufragio
wreck

la nave espacial
spacecraft

negro (m)
negra (f)
black

el nenúfar
waterlily

el neumático
tyre

la niebla
mist

el nido
nest

la nieve
snow

el nomo
gnome

nuevo (m)
nueva (f)
new

los números
numbers

Oo

Pp

el obrero
builder

el ojal
buttonhole

la ola
wave

la olla
cauldron

el ordenador
computer

las orejeras
ear muffs

la orilla del río
river bank

la ostra
oyster

el otoño
autumn

la oveja
sheep

la paja
straw

el pájaro
bird
los pájaros de jardin
garden birds

la pala
spade
la paleta
trowel

el palo de escoba
broomstick

la paloma
pigeon

el pan
bread

la pantalla de lámpara
lampshade

el pañuelo
handkerchief

el papel higiénico
toilet paper

la papelera
rubbish bin

la papelera
wastepaper bin

el paquete
parcel

el para-brisas
windscreen

el paracaidas
parachute

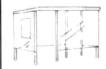
la parada de autobús cubierta
shelter

la parada del autobus
bus stop

el parapeto
windbreak

la parte de arriba
top

la parte de abajo
bottom

47

Aa Bb Cc Dd Ee Ff Gg Hh Ii Jj Kk Ll Mm Nn Oo Pp Qq Rr Ss Tt Uu Vv Ww Xx Yy Zz

el parterre
border

el parterre
flower bed

el paso de zebra
crossing

la pasta dentífrica
toothpaste

el pastel
cake

la pata
paw

la patata
potato

las patatas fritas
chips

las patatas fritas
crisps

los patines
roller skates

el patinete
skateboard

el patito
duckling
el pato
duck

el payaso
clown

el pedal
pedal

el pelaje
fur

el pelicano
pelican

la pelota de tenis
tennis ball

la pelota de playa
beach ball

el pepino
cucumber

pequeño (m)
pequeña (f)
short

la pera
pear

la percha
hanger

el periódico
newspaper

el periquito
budgerigar

el perrito caliente
hot dog

el perro pastor
sheepdog

el pescador de caña
angler

el pez-espada
swordfish

el picnic
picnic

el pico
beak

el pijama
pyjamas

la pimienta
pepper

el pincel
paintbrush

la pintura
paint

el pirata
pirate

la pista de tenis
tennis court

la pizarra
chalkboard

la plasticina
Plasticine

el plátano
banana

el plato
plate

el plato de papel
paper plate

la playa
beach

las playeras
plimsoll

la pluma
plume

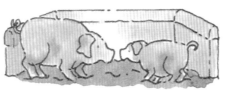
la pocilga
pig sty

el policía (m)
police officer

el pollito
chick

el poste de telégrafos
telegraph pole

el potro
foal

el poyete de la ventana
windowsill

la primavera
primrose

la primavera
spring

la príncesa
princess

el príncipe
prince

el profesor (m)
la profesora (f)
teacher

el puente
bridge

la puerta
gate

la puerta trasera
back door

el pulpo
octopus

el puño
cuff

púrpura/violeta
purple

el puzle
jigsaw puzzle

Qq

el queso
cheese

Rr

el radiador
radiator

la radio
radio

la rama
branch

el rastrillo
garden fork

el rastrillo
rake

la raya
ray fish

el rectángulo
rectangle

la red
net

la red metálica
wire netting

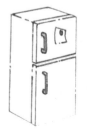
el refrigerador
fridge

el regalo
present

la regla
ruler

la reina
queen

el reloj de pared
clock

el reloj de pulsera
watch

el remo
oar

el remolque
trailer

la repisa de la chimenea
mantlepiece

la revista
magazine

el rey
king

el rinoceronte
rhinoceros

el río
river

el roble
oak tree

rojo (m)
roja (f)
red

rosa
pink

la rosa
rose

la rueda
wheel

Ss

la sábana
sheet

la sal
salt

Aa Bb Cc Dd Ee Ff Gg Hh Ii Jj Kk Ll Mm Nn Oo Pp Qq Rr Ss Tt Uu Vv Ww Xx Yy Zz

la sandalia
sandal

la sartén
frying pan

el semáforo
traffic lights

la serpentina
streamer

la serpiente
snake

la servilleta de papel
paper napkin

la seta venenosa
toadstool

la silla
chair

la silla de ruedas
wheelchair

la sillita
pushchair

el sillón
armchair

el sofá
settee

el sol
sun

el sombrero
hat

el sombrero de copa
top hat

la sombrilla
umbrella

el sonajero
rattle

la sopa
soup

la sorpresa Navideña
cracker

la sudadera
sweatshirt

el suelo de baldosas
floor tile

el sujeta-velas
candlestick

el supermercado
supermarket

Tt

la tabla de surf
surfboard

la tabla de windsurf
windsurfer

el taburete
stool

la taladradora
pneumatic drill

el tambor
drum

el tapón
plug

la tarjeta de felicitación
card

la tarjeta nemotécnica
flashcard

la televisión
television

el tenedor
fork

el tentáculo
tentacle

el termo
Thermos flask

el ternero
calf

el terrazo
terrace

el tesoro
treasure

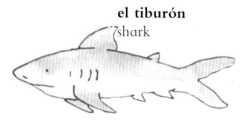
el tiburón
shark

la tienda
shop

el terraplén
slope

la tienda de campaña
tent

la tienda de juguete
toy shop

el tiesto
flowerpot

el tigre
tiger

las tijeras
scissors

el tio-vivo
roundabout

los tirantes
braces

la tiza
chalk

la toalla de baño
bath towel

la toalla de baño
flannel

la toalla de playa
beach towel

el toallero
towel rail

el tobogán
slide

el tocadiscos
record player

el tocón (de árb
tree stump

el todo-terreno
van

el tomate
tomato

la tormenta
rain shower

el toro
bull

la tortuga
tortoise

la tortuga marin
turtle

el tostador de pan
toaster

el tractor
tractor

el tractor nivelador
bulldozer

el traje de buceador
wet suit

el tren
train

el trencecito de juguete
train set

el triángulo
triangle

el triciclo
tricycle

el trineo
sledge

triste
sad

la trompa
trunk

el tubo
tube

el tubo respirador
snorkel

el tunel
tunnel

Uu

el unicornio
unicorn

la uva
grape

Vv

la vaca
cow

el vagón
carriage

los vaqueros
jeans

la varita mágica
magic wand

el vaso de papel
paper cup

la vela
candle

la vela
sail

la venda
bandage

la ventana
window

53

el ventilador
fan

la ventosa
sucker

el verano
summer

verde
green

el vertedero
skip

el vestido
dress

el vestido de fiesta
party dress

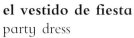

los vestidos de muñeca
doll's clothes

viejo (m)
vieja (f)
old

el vinagre
vinegar

el volante
steering wheel

Ww

el wáter
toilet

Xx

el xilófono
xylophone

Yy

el yate
yacht

el yo-yo
yo-yo

Zz

las zapatillas de casa
slipper

las zapatillas de deporte
trainers

el zapato
shoe

la zarpa
claw

la zebra
zebra

el zumo
juice

Parts of the body

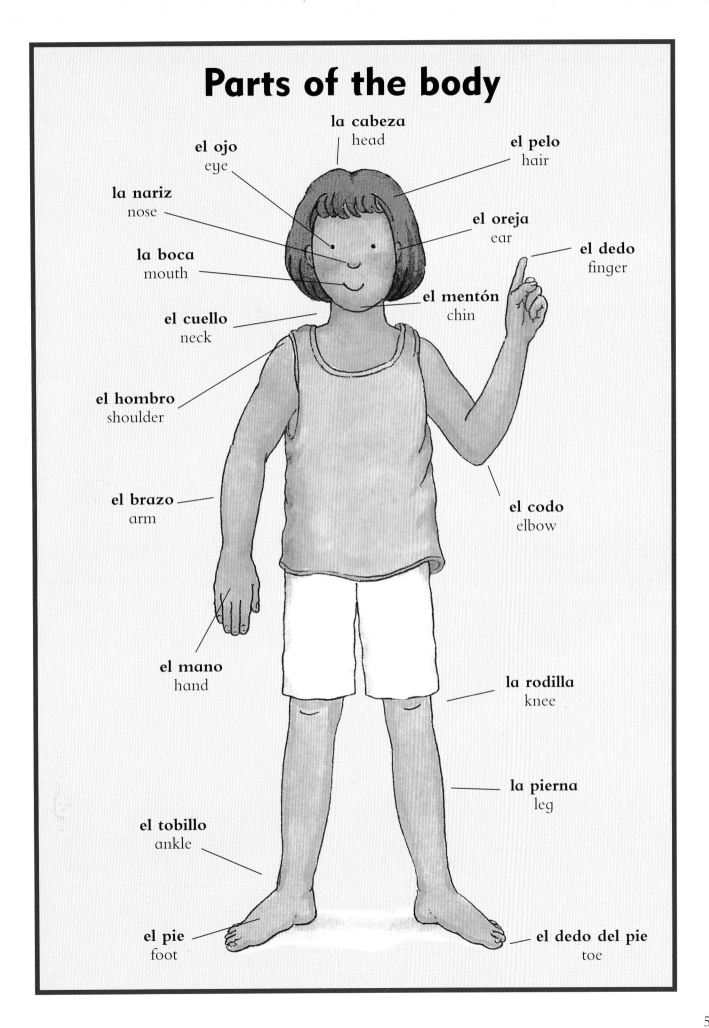

la cabeza
head

el ojo
eye

el pelo
hair

la nariz
nose

el oreja
ear

la boca
mouth

el dedo
finger

el cuello
neck

el mentón
chin

el hombro
shoulder

el brazo
arm

el codo
elbow

el mano
hand

la rodilla
knee

la pierna
leg

el tobillo
ankle

el pie
foot

el dedo del pie
toe

Los días de la semana
Days of the week

lunes	**martes**	**miércoles**	**jueves**	**viernes**
Monday	Tuesday	Wednesday	Thursday	Friday

sábado	**domingo**	**el fin de semana**
Saturday	Sunday	the weekend

Los meses del año
Months of the year

enero	**abril**	**julio**	**octubre**
January	April	July	October
febrero	**mayo**	**agosto**	**noviembre**
February	May	August	November
marzo	**junio**	**septiembre**	**diciembre**
March	June	September	December

1	**2**	**3**	**4**	**5**	**6**	**7**	**8**	**9**	**10**
uno	dos	tres	cuatro	cinco	seis	siete	ocho	nueve	diez

11	**12**	**13**	**14**	**15**	**16**	**17**	**18**	**19**	**20**
once	doce	trece	catorce	quince	dieciseis	diecisiete	dieciocho	diecinueve	veinte

21	**22**	**23**	**24**	**25**
ventiuno	ventidos	ventitres	venticuatro	venticinco

30	**40**	**50**	**60**	**70**	**80**	**90**
treinta	cuarenta	cincuenta	sesenta	setenta	ochenta	noventa

100	**1,000**	**1,000,000**
cien	mil	un millón